YOUR KNOWLEDGE HAS VALUE

The Relation between Impoliteness and Humor in "The Big Bang Theory"

Timmy Paul

Bibliographic information published by the German National Library:

The German National Library lists this publication in the National Bibliography; detailed bibliographic data are available on the Internet at http://dnb.dnb.de.

ISBN: 9783346579768
This book is also available as an ebook.

Print and binding: Books on Demand GmbH, Norderstedt, Germany
Printed on acid-free paper from responsible sources.

The present work has been carefully prepared. Nevertheless, authors and publishers do not incur liability for the correctness of information, notes, links and advice as well as any printing errors.

GRIN web shop: https://www.grin.com/document/1169259

Technische Universität Braunschweig

Fakultät für Geistes- und Erziehungswissenschaften

Englisches Seminar

Englische Sprachwissenschaft

Introduction to Pragmatics

Sommersemester 2016

The Relation between Impoliteness and Humor in

The Big Bang Theory

Name: Timmy Paul

Studiengang: 2-Fach-Bachelor English Studies und Geschichte

Fachsemester: 7.

Inhaltsverzeichnis

1. Abstract

This research paper focuses mainly on the relationship between impoliteness and humor in comedy series. In the following I will name the research questions I'm dealing with in this paper. What makes the character Sheldon Cooper a funny character? How is it possible for an almost misanthropic character like him to create humor and to entertain an audience? What are the reasons for his impolite nature and in what way are they presented? My hypothesis is that *The Big Bang Theory* uses impoliteness and power relations to create a specific type of humor, which is able to make even an antisocial character likable and congenial. In order to test my hypothesis, I reviewed the Politeness Strategies by Brown and Levinson (1978) and the Impoliteness Strategies by Culpeper (2005). Furthermore I made researches about the connection between power and impoliteness and their relation to humor. During the procedure I matched the received information with inserted data from the sitcom in order to learn about their effects on spectators. Based on the findings I received during my research, one can say that the combination of impoliteness and power leads under specific conditions to amusement and enjoyment within the audience. Taking into account different factors, can turn an offensive utterance or even a conflict between two or more people into a tool of humor and thus cause delight for observers. The main conclusions of this paper are, that Sheldon Cooper's behavior perfectly matches the Impoliteness Strategies by Culpeper (2005), that power plays a significant role in creating impoliteness and that impoliteness and conflict are strongly connected to humor.

2. Introduction

Today's tv program is dominated by a variety of different genres. A special kind of comedy for example is the sitcom. There are a lot of sitcoms nowadays and more are upcoming. Most of them use impoliteness, rude behavior and conflict between the characters as trigger for humor. Comedy series like these use different locations, plots and a variety of characters to create as many opportunities to create humor as possible. The example I use in this paper is the sitcom *The Big Bang Theory*, especially the character of Sheldon Cooper, who is most of the time depicted as an antisocial and impolite person.

In my view the importance lies in the analysis of which communication systems Sheldon uses and which not and what the results on the audience are. Furthermore I want to concentrate on the combination of impoliteness and humor and therefore clarify which specific mechanics can turn an offensive statement, which would normally cause confusion or anger, into a witty situation. I will do so by analysing different views on politeness and impoliteness, their definitions, different communication models and the behavior of Sheldon Cooper in specific scenes of *The Big Bang Theory*. I expect to obtain new knowledge about the topic of humor in contemporary times. Over time the meaning of humor in the media has changed. In my opinion the research about contemporary humor is important since *The Big Bang Theory* is not the only comedy TV show, that relies on somehow odd, rude and antisocial characters.

My research paper is partitioned into multiple subjects. In the following sections, I will give an overview of different definitions of linguistic humor, politeness and impoliteness. Furthermore I will give an insight into two different communication systems (Brown & Levinson, Culpeper). In the later sections I will discuss the connection between power and impoliteness and the effects of impoliteness on humor.

3. Definition of Linguistic Humor, Politeness and Impoliteness

3.1 Linguistic Humor

According to Attardo (1994) more than once it has been claimed that there is no specific definition of humor in general. Many researchers see the lack of a definition of humor as an obstacle for researching fields like irony and satire. In fact it is rather unclear what counts as humor. A few attempts were made to explain this phenomenon. Oswald Ducrot and Tzvetan Todorov (Ducrot & Todorov, 1972; as cited in Attardo, 1994) explain in their approach for example, that the literary genre of comedy has to be differentiated from the general category of the comic.

Other linguists declared that any event that causes laughing or amusement can be seen as humor. Victor Raskin (Raskin, 1985; as cited in Attardo, 1994) describes it as the least restricted sense. Gourévitch (Gourévitch, 1975; as cited in Attardo, 1994) defines comedy as "a miscellaneous genre activated by a plurality of impulses: for example farce, humor, satire and irony."

Furthermore there were many attemps to subcategorize and differentiate humor and its subfields on their basis, for example sexual, aggressive or scatological, which was denied by a number of researchers. Moreover there is no explicit distinction of humor in reality and the translatability of the author's terminology can hinder further research. Interdiciplinary issues are caused because researchers of diverse diciplines are defining comedy and jokes differently.

3.2 Politeness, Nonpoliteness and Impoliteness according to Leech

According to Geoffrey Leech (2014), there are eight characteristics, which express and shape the entity of politeness. First of all, he explains that politeness is not obligatory. Rude behavior or impoliteness can occur at any occasion and without any reason. There also are different gradations of politeness and impoliteness, like bowing and clapping. He also mentiones "the sense of what is normal". This means that members of a specific society recognize what an appropriate gesture of politeness for a particular occasion is.

Furthermore he argues that it depends on the situation wheter politeness will occur or not and when. He also mentiones the "reciprocal asymmetry" between two parties, which means that if party B observes a polite gesture by party A, party B has to give high value to party A or to attribute low value to him or herself in order to act polite. Another characteristic of politeness according to Leech (2014) is that politeness can manifest itself in repetitive behavior. This means that polite behavior can be ritualized like applause after a concert for example.

Moreover we experience a "transaction of value" due to acting in a polite manner. Speech acts like compliments, thanks, apologies and invitations involve such transactions for example. The last characteristic of politeness according to Leech

(2014) is, its tendency to preserve a balance of value between two parties.

Nonpoliteness excludes politeness values of any kind. That means that nonpolite utterances lack both politeness and impoliteness. Furthermore it can be distinguished between nonpoliteness in a pragmalinguistic sense and nonpoliteness in a sociolinguistic sense. Despite the fact that politeness is closely related to it, impoliteness can not be compared to it and has to be analysed under its own condititions.

According to Jonathan Culpeper (Culpeper, 1996; as cited in Leech, 2014) impoliteness can either be characterized as face attack that is intentionally uttered by a speaker, as the hearer's perception that one's behavior is an intentional face attack or even as combination of both. Nowadays it can not be doubted that in some specific situations, impoliteness can indeed be humorous. It can be observed that impoliteness exposed in TV programs can trigger amusement within the audience, since the observer's own face is not threatened in any way.

3.3 Politeness Strategies by Penelope Brown and Stephen C. Levinson

Penelope Brown and Stephen C. Levinson (1978) describe in their approach to politeness the system of "Face-Threatening Acts", the so called FTAs. The notion of "face" is very apparent within the theory. Brown and Levinson's concept of face derives from Goffman's politeness theory and is connected to the idea of "losing and keeping face". The theory describes that the face of a person can be threatened, but also repaired. The concept is based on the notion that every participant's has the interest to mantain each others face, in order to protect their own face. Furthermore face can be considered as basic want.

In this context, Brown and Levinson (1978) introduce the Face-Threatening-Act-System (FTA-System). The system gives the speaker the choice between doing the FTA or refraining from doing so. If the speaker choses to perform the FTA, he or she can do it off record (indirectly) or on record. Doing the FTA off record intends to not impose inconveniences on the hearer. If it is performed on record, it can be executed without redressive action (baldly), which does not intend to reduce the threat to the hearer's face or with redressive action. If it is performed with redressive action it can be executed with positive politeness, which is used to give the hearer a feeling of closeness and belonging, or with negative politeness, which is used to communicate with the hearer in a non-imposing way.

3.4 Impoliteness Strategies by Jonathan Culpeper

In contrast to this, Jonathan Culpeper's Model of Impoliteness (2005) contains various strategies that might look similar to Brown and Levinson's approach but actually are not. Culpeper's model comes up with similar terms but they carry his own specific ideas.

For example his model introduces the Bald on Record Impoliteness to us, which means that "the FTA is performed in a direct, clear, unambiguous and concise way in circumstances where face is not irrelevant or minimized." (Culpeper, 2005, p.

41).

Positive Impoliteness is described as followed:

> The use of strategies designed to damage the addressee's positive face wants, e.g. Ignore, snub the other - fail to acknowledge the other's presence. Exclude the other from an activity. Disassociate from the other - for example, deny association or common ground with the other; avoid sitting together. Be disinterested, unconcerned, unsympathetic. Use inappropriate identity markers - for example, use title and surname when a close relationship pertains, or a nickname when a distant relationship pertains. Use obscure or secretive language - for example, mystify the other with jargon, or use a code known to others in the group, but not the target. Seek disagreement - select a sensitive topic. Make the other feel uncomfortable - for example, do not avoid silence, joke, or use small talk. Use taboo words - swear, or use abusive or profane language. Call the other names - use derogatory nominations. (Culpeper, 2005, p. 41).

The strategy of Negative Impoliteness is introduced as followed:

> The use of strategies designed to damage the addressee's negative face wants, e.g. Frighten - instill a belief that action detrimental to the other will occur. Condescend, scorn or ridicule - emphasize your relative power. Be contemptuous. Do not treat the other seriously. Belittle the other (e.g. use diminutives). Invade the other's space - literally (e.g. position yourself closer to the other than the relationship permits) or metaphorically (e.g. ask for or speak about information which is too intimate given the relationship). Explicitly associate the other with a negative aspect - personalize, use the pronouns 'I' and 'you'. Put the other's indebtedness on record. Violate the structure of conversation – interrupt. (Culpeper, 2005, p. 41).

Using the Off-Record Impoliteness means that "The FTA is performed by means of an implicature but in such a way that one attributable intention clearly outweighs any others." (Culpeper, 2005, p. 44).

Moreover there is the strategy of Withholding Politeness which means that "The absence of politeness work[s] where it would be expected. For example, failing to thank somebody for a present may be taken as deliberate impoliteness." (Culpeper, 2005, p. 42).

Using the act of Sarcasm or Mock Politeness means that "The FTA is performed with the use of politeness strategies that are obviously insincere, and thus remain surface realisations." (Culpeper, 2005, p. 42).

4. Data and Analysis of Specific Conversational Fragments, Jokes and Punchlines from *The Big Bang Theory*

Taken from: *The Big Bang Theory*, Season 1, Episode 08.

Sheldon: Sorry I'm late.

Leonard: What happened?

Sheldon: Nothing, I just really didn't want to come. Virgin diet cuba libre please.

In this conversational fragment, Sheldon clearly flouts the politeness system by Brown and Levinson (1978). Instead his behavior can be put into words by one of Culpeper's Impoliteness Strategies (2005). Sheldon makes use of the Bald on Record Impoliteness strategy by telling Leonard in a clear, concise and unambiguous manner, that he had no interest in joining him and Penny. There is no hint that he intends to threaten Leonards positive or negative face but he does not hestitate although face is not irrelevant in this situation.

Taken from: *The Big Bang Theory*, Season 4, Episode 01.

Penny: Can I ask you a question?

Sheldon: Given your community college education, I encourage you to ask me as many as possible.

In this example, Penny implies that she wants to ask Sheldon a question. Instead of an expected polite reaction, he uses Positive Impoliteness to attack Penny's positive face wants. He snubs her in a direct and unsympathetic way by implying that she is unusually low educated, despite the fact that she just asks him a simple and neutral question. The impact is especially severe because Penny is self-concious about her level of education.

Taken from: *The Big Bang Theory*, Season 4, Episode 24.

Priya: Uh, I'll have the Shepherd's Pie. You want to split that with me?

Leonard: Oh, no, no, no, he doesn't.

Priya: Why not?

Leonard: Well, you have milk in the taters, milk in the gravy, parmesan crust. Your lactose-intolerant boyfriend will turn into a gas-filled Macy's Day balloon.

Sheldon: Not quite accurate. The Macy's balloons are filled with helium, whereas Leonard produces copious amounts of methane.

In this fragment, Sheldon makes use of the strategy of Negative Impoliteness. It is obvious that Sheldon makes an effort to attack Leonards negative face wants. First of all, when Leonard and Priya are having a conversation, Sheldon interferes. This can already be seen as impolite, since Leonard and Priya are obviously talking about a sensitive topic. Secondly he affronts Leonard in front of Priya by broadening the conversation about the negative effects of Leonards lactose-intolerance, making it inappropriate and inconvenient.

Taken from: *The Big Bang Theory*, Season 02, Episode 16.

Leonard: Don't sit in his spot.

Penny: Fine. *(Moves)* Happy?

Sheldon: I'm not unhappy.

This is an example for Sheldon using the strategy of Withholding Politeness. The audience expects at least a kind reaction, like an acknowledgement by Sheldon. Instead he flouts this expectation by withholding a polite answer. This can clearly be seen as intended impoliteness.

Taken from: *The Big Bang Theory*, Season 02, Episode 20.

Howard: Come on, the whole idea behind Anything Can Happen Thursday is to get out of this rut we've been in lately.

Sheldon: Rut? I think you mean consistency. And if we're going to abandon that, then why even call it Thursday? Let's call it Quonko Day and divide it into 29 hours of 17 minutes apiece, and celebrate it by sacrificing a goat to the mighty god Ra.

In this conversational fragment, Sheldon uses the Impoliteness Meta-Strategy, Sarcasm or Mock-Politeness, in order to snub his friends. In a doubtless manner, he makes clear that he is against the idea of "Anything Can Happen Thursday", by making obviously exaggerated and thus insincere suggestions concerning this matter.

5. Power and Impoliteness in *The Big Bang Theory*

The aspect of power can be seen as a crucial factor in the context of impolite behavior. Every time somebody makes use of impoliteness, power somehow plays a significant role, since impoliteness can be seen as a display of power. In general, one can observe that impoliteness is often used by more powerful individuals towards a less powerful addressee.

In *The Big Bang Theory*, Sheldon consideres himself as the most intelligent person and thus the most powerful in the entire series. As a result the audience can observe scenes like those described in the section before. Sheldon is obviously aware of the fact that his intelligence is extraordinary, what causes a feeling of superiority in him. Even the fact that other persons, who appear in the series, are a lot smarter than him, is not able to change this sense. This causes Sheldon's sense of superiority turn into limitless arrogance, which results in a social imbalance between him and the rest of the group.

Culpeper (1996) describes in his work, what might explain why Sheldon does not hesitate to discipline his mates when he feels to be snubbed by one of them:

> A powerful participant has more freedom to be impolite, because he or she can (a) reduce the ability of the less powerful participant to retaliate with impoliteness (e.g. through the denial of speaking rights), and (b) threaten more severe retaliation should the less powerful participant be impolite. (Culpeper, 1996, p. 354)

This clearly mirrors Sheldon's harsh behavior, if some of his friends criticise him. Usually he strikes back by verbally attacking the others face, leaving them behind critically offended and without or only covert contradiction. In order to prevent these situations, the other members of the group try to avoid any confrontation with Sheldon, what gives him power.

6. Impoliteness and Entertainment

According to Culpeper (2011) the humor creating effect of sitcoms like *The Big Bang Theory* lies in a type of impoliteness, which he describes as exploitative. Zillmann and Bryant (1994) mention in their definition that the sense of delight emerges at the misfortunes of others. Furthermore Culpeper (2011) explains that impoliteness generally amuses those, who are not target of it. According to him, the audience can experience five different kinds of pleasure, while witnessing impolite actions without being affected.

First we have the so called Emotional Pleasure, which means that spectators of violent actions, experiences an inner emotional enjoyment, for example while watching a boxing match. He then mentions the Aesthetic Pleasure. This kind of pleasure occurs when verbal creativity is used in a socially negative way. Creativity can be seen as a powerful and amusing tool for face-threatening. Next he describes the so called Voyeuristic Pleasure, which occurs while observing a conflict situation between two or more people. As an explicit example, television talk shows are mentioned in this context. Furthermore he names The Pleasure of being Superior. This idea is based on the Superiority Theory of Humor and means that amusement occurs where the audience can compare itself with less intelligent, less aesthetic or subordinate persons. The last source he mentiones, is the Pleasure of Feeling Secure. It means that the audience can feel a sense of enjoyment because it is not, who is being verbally attacked and who can watch the spectacle from a safe point of view.

7. Conclusion

In fact most of today's comedy TV series and movies are based on a type of humor, which is connected to somebody else's misfortune. It does not matter if it is Charlie Chaplin slipping on a banana peel, a so called "roast" of a celebrity or Sheldon Cooper offending his companions. They all have in common that the audience laughs at somebody else's costs. One can notice, that this kind of entertainment existed over milleniums, for example gladiator fights in ancient rome or public executions in the medieval time.

In contrast to this, the examples from *The Big Bang Theory* are actually rather harmless. Nevertheless Sheldon Cooper's face attacks are offensive, insulting and entertaining at the same time. But as I already mentioned earlier, they are only offensive and insulting towards the target, and maybe to spectators, who identify themselves with the target, whereas the rest of the audience enjoys the conflict. In my opinion, Culpeper's Five Sources of Pleasure (2011) perfectly explain, how a rude and impolite character like Sheldon Cooper is able to create humor and to entertain an audience.

Based on my research, Sheldon's impolite behavior can be put into words by Culpeper's Model of Impoliteness (2005), which contrasts Brown and Levinson's Model of Politeness (1987) and helps us to understand how Sheldon's utterances can be classified and interpreted.

The reason for his impolite nature obviously lays in his arrogant character, emerging from his notion of superiority towards his friends, which derives from his in fact extraordinary intelligence. He even acts impolite towards people, who are clearly more intelligent than him, which is a fact, he simply refuses. The notion of superiority leads us to the concept of power. As I already mentioned, Culpeper (2011) decribes, that power may lead to impoliteness, since this is a tool of demonstrating it.

The subject of this paper can be deepened in further papers by analysing and comparing different kinds of comedy series, in order to learn more about today's humor and it's tendencies. It is interesting to see, where this kind of humor derived from and how it changed over time. It seems to be interesting to investigate, where the sense of pleasure we experience on somebody else's costs, comes from and what the reasons for this are. In my view, these findings can lead into an in-depth research, not only on humor, but also on the human behavior and psychology.

List of references

- Attardo, S. (1994). *Linguistic Theories of Humor.* Berlin: Mouton de Gruyter.
- Brown, P. & Levinson S. (1978). *Politeness.* Cambridge: Cambridge University Press.
- Bryant, J. & Zillmann, D. (1994). *Media Effects: Advances in Theory and Research.* Hillsdale: Lawrence Erlbaum Associates.
- Culpeper, J. (1996). Towards an Anatomy of Impoliteness. *Journal of Pragmatics, 25*(3), 349-367.
- Culpeper, J. (2005). Impoliteness and Entertainment in The Television Quiz Show: 'The Weakest Link'. *Journal of Politeness Research, 1*(1), 35-72.
- Culpeper, J. (2011). *Impoliteness: Using Language to Cause Offence.* Cambridge: Cambridge University Press.
- Ducrot, O. & Todorov, T. (1972). *Dictionnaire encyclopédique des sciences du langage.* Paris: Éditions du Seuil.
- Gourévitch, J. (1975). *Comprendre la publicité.* Paris: Editions de l'Ecole.
- Leech, G. (2014). *The Pragmatics of Politeness.* New York: Oxford University Press.
- Lorre, C. (2007). *The Big Bang Theory.* Retrieved 09.01.2017, from https://bigbangtrans.wordpress.com/
- Raskin, V. (1985). *Semantic Mechanisms of Humor.* Dordrecht: D. Reidel Publishing Company.

YOUR KNOWLEDGE HAS VALUE

- We will publish your bachelor's and
  master's thesis, essays and papers

- Your own eBook and book -
  sold worldwide in all relevant shops

- Earn money with each sale

Upload your text at www.GRIN.com
and publish for free